Routers, including: Router, Cisco Ios, Pe Router, Netgear, Gateway (telecommunications), Wireless Router Application Platform, Cellular Router, Vyatta, Router Clustering, Passport Carrier Release, Core Router, Waav, Inc., Routing Control Plane, Untangle

Hephaestus Books

Contents

Articles

References

Router

Router

A **router** is an electronic device that interconnects two or more computer networks, and selectively interchanges packets of data between them. Each data packet contains address information that a router can use to determine if the source and destination are on the same network, or if the data packet must be transferred from one network to another. When multiple routers are used in a large collection of interconnected networks, the routers exchange information about target system addresses, so that each router can build up a table showing the preferred paths between any two systems on the interconnected networks.

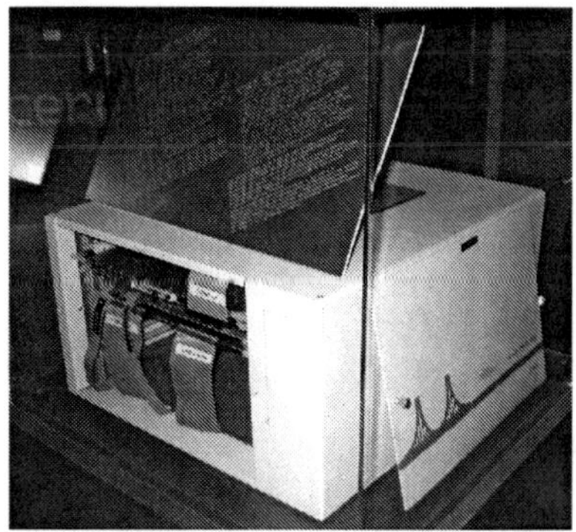

A Cisco ASM/2-32EM router deployed at CERN in 1987.

A router is a networking device whose software and hardware are customized to the tasks of routing and forwarding information. A router has two or more network interfaces, which may be to different physical types of network (such as copper cables, fiber, or wireless) or different network standards. Each network interface is a specialized device that converts electric signals from one form to another.

Juniper SRX210 service gateway router

Routers connect two or more logical subnets, each having a different network address. The subnets in the router do not necessarily map one-to-one to the physical interfaces of the router. The term "layer 3 switching" is often used interchangeably with the term "routing". The term switching is generally used to refer to data forwarding between two network devices with the same network address. This is also called layer 2 switching or LAN switching.

Conceptually, a router operates in two operational planes (or sub-systems):

- Control plane: where a router builds a table (called routing table) as how a packet should be forwarded through which interface, by using either statically configured statements (called static routes) or by exchanging information with other routers in the network through a dynamical routing protocol;

- Forwarding plane: where the router actually forwards traffic (called packets in IP) from ingress (incoming) interfaces to an egress (outgoing) interface that is appropriate for the destination address that the packet carries with it, by following rules derived from the routing table that has been built in the control plane.

Types of routers

Routers may provide connectivity inside enterprises, between enterprises and the Internet, and inside internet service providers (ISPs). The largest routers (for example the Cisco CRS-1 or Juniper T1600) interconnect ISPs, are used inside ISPs, or may be used in very large enterprise networks. The smallest routers provide connectivity for small and home offices.

Routers for Internet connectivity and internal use

Routers intended for ISP and major enterprise connectivity almost invariably exchange routing information using the Border Gateway Protocol (BGP). RFC 4098 defines several types of BGP-speaking routers according to the routers' functions:

- *Edge router* (ER): An ER is placed at the edge of an ISP network. The router speaks external BGP (EBGP) to a BGP speaker in another provider or large enterprise Autonomous System(AS). This type of router is also called PE (Provider Edge) routers.
- *Subscriber edge router* (SER): An SER is located at the edge of the subscriber's network, it speaks EBGP to its provider's AS(s). It belongs to an end user (enterprise) organization. This type of router is also called CE (Customer Edge) routers.
- *Inter-provider border router*: Interconnecting ISPs, this is a BGP-speaking router that maintains BGP sessions with other BGP speaking routers in other providers' ASes.
- Core router: A *core router* is one that resides within an AS as back bone to carry traffic between edge routers.

  Within an ISP: Internal to the provider's AS, such a router speaks internal BGP (IBGP) to that provider's edge routers, other intra-provider core routers, or the provider's inter-provider border routers.

  "Internet backbone:" The Internet does not have a clearly identifiable backbone, as did its predecessors. See default-free zone (DFZ). Nevertheless, the major ISPs' routers make up what many would consider the core. These ISPs operate all four types of the BGP-speaking routers described here. In ISP usage, a "core" router is internal to an ISP, and used to interconnect its edge and border routers. Core routers may also have specialized functions in virtual private networks based on a combination of BGP and Multi-Protocol Label Switching (MPLS).

Routers are also used for port forwarding for private servers.

History

Leonard Kleinrock and the first IMP.

The very first device that had fundamentally the same functionality as a router does today, i.e a packet switch, was the Interface Message Processor (IMP); IMPs were the devices that made up the ARPANET, the first packet switching network. The idea for a router (although they were called "gateways" at the time) initially came about through an international group of computer networking researchers called the International Network Working Group (INWG). Set up in 1972 as an informal group to consider the technical issues involved in connecting different networks, later that year it became a subcommittee of the International Federation for Information Processing.

These devices were different from most previous packet switches in two ways. First, they connected dissimilar kinds of networks, such as serial lines and local area networks. Second, they were connectionless devices, which had no role in assuring that traffic was delivered reliably, leaving that entirely to the hosts (although this particular idea had been previously pioneered in the CYCLADES network).

The idea was explored in more detail, with the intention to produce a real prototype system, as part of two contemporaneous programs. One was the initial DARPA-initiated program, which created the TCP/IP architecture of today. The other was a program at Xerox PARC to explore new networking technologies, which produced the PARC Universal Packet system, although due to corporate intellectual property concerns it received little attention outside Xerox until years later.

The earliest Xerox routers came into operation sometime after early 1974. The first true IP router was developed by Virginia Strazisar at BBN, as part of that DARPA-initiated effort, during 1975-1976. By the end of 1976, three PDP-11-based routers were in service in the experimental prototype Internet.

The first multiprotocol routers were independently created by staff researchers at MIT and Stanford in 1981; the Stanford router was done by William Yeager, and the MIT one by Noel Chiappa; both were also based on PDP-11s.

As virtually all networking now uses IP at the network layer, multiprotocol routers are largely obsolete, although they were important in the early stages of the growth of computer networking, when several protocols other than TCP/IP were in widespread use. Routers that handle both IPv4 and IPv6 arguably are multiprotocol, but in a far less variable sense than a router that processed AppleTalk, DECnet, IP, and Xerox protocols.

In the original era of routing (from the mid-1970s through the 1980s), general-purpose mini-computers served as routers. Although general-purpose computers can perform routing, modern high-speed routers are highly specialized computers, generally with extra hardware added to accelerate both common routing functions, such as packet forwarding and specialised functions such as IPsec encryption.

Still, there is substantial use of Linux and Unix machines, running open source routing code, for routing research and other applications. While Cisco's operating system was independently designed, other major router operating systems, such as those from Juniper Networks and Extreme Networks, are extensively modified but still have Unix ancestry.

Enterprise routers

All sizes of routers may be found inside enterprises. The most powerful routers tend to be found in ISPs and academic & research facilities. Large businesses may also need powerful routers.

A three-layer model is in common use, not all of which need be present in smaller networks.

Access

Access routers, including 'small office/home office' (SOHO) models, are located at customer sites such as branch offices that do not need hierarchical routing of their own. Typically, they are optimized for low cost. Some SOHO routers are capable of running alternative free Linux-based firmwares like OpenWrt.

Linksys by Cisco WRT54GL SoHo Router

Distribution

Distribution routers aggregate traffic from multiple access routers, either at the same site, or to collect the data streams from multiple sites to a major enterprise location. Distribution routers often are responsible for enforcing quality of service across a WAN, so they may have considerable memory, multiple WAN interfaces, and substantial processing intelligence.

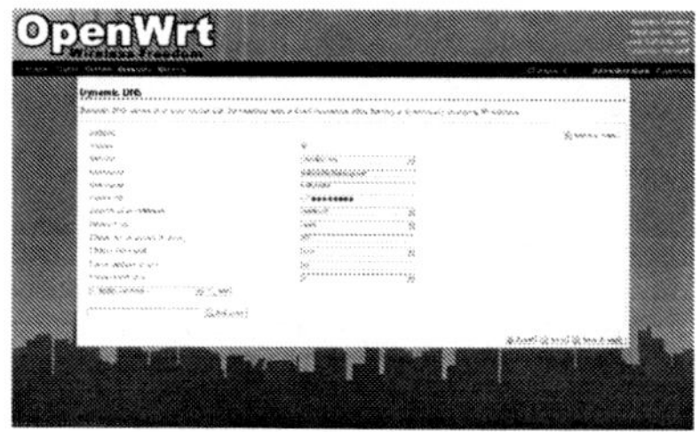

A screenshot of the LuCI web interface used by OpenWrt. Here it is being used to configure Dynamic DNS.

They may also provide connectivity to groups of servers or to external networks. In the latter application, the router's functionality must be carefully considered as part of the overall security architecture. Separate from the router may be a firewall or VPN concentrator, or the router may include these and other security functions.

Core

In enterprises, a core router may provide a "collapsed backbone" interconnecting the distribution tier routers from multiple buildings of a campus, or large enterprise locations. They tend to be optimized for high bandwidth.

When an enterprise is widely distributed with no central location(s), the function of core routing may be subsumed by the WAN service to which the enterprise subscribes, and the distribution routers become the highest tier.

Forwarding plane (a.k.a. data plane)

Main article: Forwarding plane

For pure Internet Protocol (IP) forwarding function, a router is designed to minimize the state information on individual packets. A router does not look into the actual data contents that the packet carries, but only at the layer 3 addresses to make a forwarding decision, plus optionally other information in the header for hint on, for example, QoS. Once a packet is forwarded, the router does not retain any historical information about the packet, but the forwarding action can be collected into the statistical data, if so configured.

Forwarding decisions can involve decisions at layers other than the IP internetwork layer or OSI layer 3. A function that forwards based on data link layer, or OSI layer 2, information, is properly called a bridge or switch. This function is referred to as layer 2 switching, as the addresses it uses to forward the traffic are layer 2 addresses in the OSI layer model.

Besides making decision as which interface a packet is forwarded to, which is handled primarily via the routing table, a router also has to manage congestion, when packets arrive at a rate higher than the router can process. Three policies commonly used in the Internet are tail drop, random early detection, and weighted random early detection. Tail drop is the simplest and most easily implemented; the router simply drops packets once the length of the queue exceeds the size of the buffers in the router. Random early detection (RED) probabilistically drops datagrams early when the queue is about to exceed a pre-configured size of the queue. Weighted random early detection requires a weight on the average queue size to act upon when the traffic is about to exceed the pre-configured size, so that short bursts will not trigger random drops.

Another function a router performs is to decide which packet should be processed first when multiple queues exist. This is managed through QoS (Quality of Service), which is critical when VoIP (Voice over IP) is deployed, so that delays between packets do not exceed 150ms to maintain the quality of voice conversations.

Yet another function a router performs is called "policy based routing" where special rules are constructed to override the rules derived from the routing table when a packet forwarding decision is made.

These functions may be performed through the same internal paths that the packets travel inside the router. Some of the functions may be performed through an application-specific integrated circuit (ASIC) to avoid overhead caused by multiple CPU cycles, and others may have to be performed through the CPU as these packets need special attention that cannot be handled by an ASIC.

Router Manufacturers

The major router manufacturers include:

- Alcatel-Lucent
- Asus
- Avaya
- Belkin
- Brocade
- Buffalo
- Cisco Systems
- D-link
- Extreme Networks
- Fujitsu
- Huawei
- Juniper Networks
- Netgear
- TP-Link
- UTStarcom
- ZTE
- ZyXEL

External links

- Internet Engineering Task Force, the Routing Area [1]
- Internet Corporation for Assigned Names and Numbers [2]
- North American Network Operators Group [3]
- Réseaux IP Européens (European IP Networks) [4]
- American Registry for Internet Numbers [5]
- Asia-Pacific Network Information Center [6]
- Latin American Network Information Center [7]
- African Region Internet Registry [8]
- Wireless Network Switching Subsystem [9]
- Network router cheat sheet [10]

Cisco IOS

Cisco IOS

Company / developer	Cisco Systems
Working state	Current
Source model	Closed source
Latest stable release	15.0(1)M / October 2, 2009
Available language(s)	English
Supported platforms	The majority of Cisco routers and current Cisco switches
Default user interface	Command line interface
Official website	Cisco IOS [1]

Cisco IOS (originally **Internetwork Operating System**) is the software used on the vast majority of Cisco Systems routers and current Cisco network switches. *(Earlier switches ran CatOS.)* IOS is a package of routing, switching, internetworking and telecommunications functions tightly integrated with a multitasking operating system.

Cisco IOS has a characteristic command line interface (CLI), whose style has been widely copied by other networking products. The IOS CLI provides a fixed set of multiple-word commands — the set available is determined by the "mode" and the privilege level of the current user. "Global configuration mode" provides commands to change the system's configuration, and "interface configuration mode" provides commands to change the configuration of a specific interface. All commands are assigned a *privilege level*, from 0 to 15, and can only be accessed by users with the necessary privilege. Through the CLI, the commands available to each privilege level can be defined.

Versioning

Cisco IOS is versioned using three numbers and some letters, in the general form *a.b(c.d)e*, where:

- *a* is the major version number.
- *b* is the minor version number.
- *c* is the release number, which begins at one and increments as new releases in the same *a.b* train are released.
- *d* (omitted from general releases) is the interim build number.
- *e* (zero, one or two letters) is the release train identifier, such as none (which designates the mainline, see below), *T* (for Technology), *E* (for Enterprise), *S* (for Service provider), *XA* as a special functionality train, *XB* as a different special functionality train, etc.

For example, release 12.3(1) is the first mainline Cisco IOS release of version 12.3. 12.3(2) is the next release, and so on. 12.3(1)T is the first release of the T train, 12.3(2)T the next, and so on. Interim builds are candidates for the next release, and are frequently made available by Cisco support as a faster way to provide fixes for bugs before the next release is available. For example, 12.3(1.2)T is the 2nd interim build after release 12.3(1)T.

Rebuilds - Often a rebuild is compiled to fix a single specific problem or vulnerability for a given IOS version. For example, 12.1(8)E14 is a Rebuild, the 14 denoting the 14th rebuild of 12.1(8)E. Rebuilds are produced to either quickly repair a defect, or to satisfy customers who do not want to upgrade to a later major revision because they may be running critical infrastructure on their devices, and hence prefer to minimise change and risk.

Interim releases - Are usually produced on a weekly basis, and form a roll-up of current development effort. The Cisco advisory web site may list more than one possible interim to fix an associated issue (the reason for this is unknown to the general public).

Maintenance releases - Rigorously tested releases that are made available and include enhancements and bug fixes. Cisco recommend upgrading to Maintenance releases where possible, over Interim and Rebuild releases.

Trains

Cisco IOS releases are split into several "trains", each containing a different set of features. Trains more or less map onto distinct markets or groups of customers that Cisco is targeting.

- The **mainline** train is designed to be the most stable release the company can offer, and its feature set never expands during its lifetime. Updates are released only to address bugs in the product. The previous technology train becomes the source for the current mainline train — for example, the 12.1T train becomes the basis for the 12.2 mainline. Therefore, to determine the features available in a particular mainline release, look at the previous T train release.

- The **T** - Technology train, gets new features and bug fixes throughout its life, and is therefore less stable than the mainline. (In releases prior to Cisco IOS Release 12.0, the **P** train served as the Technology train.) Cisco doesn't recommend usage of T train in production environments unless there is urgency to implement a certain T train's new IOS feature.
- The **S** - Service Provider train, runs only on the company's core router products and is heavily customized for Service Provider customers.
- The **E** - Enterprise train, is customized for implementation in enterprise environments.
- The **B** - broadband train, support internet based broadband features.
- The **X*** - *The XA, XB ... special functionality train, needs to be documented*

There are other trains from time to time, designed for specific needs — for example, the 12.0AA train contained new code required for Cisco's AS5800 product.

Packaging / feature sets

Most Cisco products that run IOS also have one or more "feature sets" or "packages", typically eight packages for Cisco routers and five packages for Cisco network switches. For example, Cisco IOS releases meant for use on Catalyst switches are available as "standard" versions (providing only basic IP routing), "enhanced" versions, which provide full IPv4 routing support, and "advanced IP services" versions, which provide the enhanced features as well as IPv6 support.

Each individual package corresponds to one service category, such as

- IP data
- Converged voice and data
- Security and VPN

For additional information about Cisco IOS Packaging see White Paper: Cisco IOS Reference Guide [2]

The exact feature set required for a particular function can be determined using the Cisco Feature Set Browser [3].

Beginning with the 1900, 2900 and 3900 series of ISR Routers, Cisco have revised the licensing model of IOS. Routers come with IP Base installed, and additional feature pack licenses can be installed as bolt-on additions to expand the feature set of the device. The available feature packs are:

- **Data** adds features like BFD, IP SLAs, IPX, L2TPv3, Mobile IP, MPLS.
- **Security** adds features like VPN, Firewall, IP SLAs, NAC.
- **Unified Comms** adds features like CallManager Express, Gatekeeper, H.323, IP SLAs, MGCP, SIP, VoIP.

Architecture

In all versions of Cisco IOS, packet routing and forwarding (switching) are distinct functions. Routing and other protocols run as Cisco IOS processes and contribute to the Routing Information Base (RIB). This is processed to generate the final IP forwarding table (FIB, Forwarding Information Base), which is used by the forwarding function of the router. On router platforms with software-only forwarding (e.g., Cisco 7200) most traffic handling, including access control list filtering and forwarding, is done at interrupt level using Cisco Express Forwarding (CEF) or dCEF (Distributed CEF). This means IOS does not have to do a process context switch to forward a packet. Routing functions such as OSPF or BGP run at the process level. In routers with hardware-based forwarding, such as the Cisco 12000 series, IOS computes the FIB in software and loads it into the forwarding hardware (such as an ASIC or network processor), which performs the actual packet forwarding function.

Cisco IOS has a "monolithic" architecture, which means that it runs as a single image and all processes share the same memory space. There is no memory protection between processes, which means that bugs in IOS code can potentially corrupt data used by other processes. It also has a *run to completion* scheduler, which means that the kernel does not pre-empt a running process — the process must make a kernel call before other processes get a chance to run. For Cisco products that required very high availability, such as the Cisco CRS-1, these limitations were not acceptable. In addition, competitive router operating systems that emerged 10–20 years after IOS, such as Juniper's JUNOS, were designed not to have these limitations. Cisco's response was to develop a new version of Cisco IOS called IOS XR that offered modularity and memory protection between processes, lightweight threads, pre-emptive scheduling and the ability to independently re-start failed processes. IOS XR uses a 3rd party real-time operating system microkernel (QNX), and a large part of the current IOS code was re-written to take advantage of the features offered by the new kernel — a massive undertaking. But the microkernel architecture removes from the kernel all processes that are not absolutely required to run in the kernel, and executes them as processes similar to the application processes. Through this method, IOS XR is able to achieve the high availability desired for the new router platform. Thus IOS and IOS XR are very different codebases, though related in functionality and design. In 2005, Cisco introduced IOS XR on the Cisco 12000 series platform, extending the microkernel architecture from the CRS-1 to Cisco's widely deployed core router.

In 2006, Cisco has made available IOS Software Modularity which extends the QNX microkernel into a more traditional IOS environment, but still providing the software upgrade capabilities that customers are demanding. It is currently available on the Catalyst 6500 enterprise switch.

Security and vulnerabilities

Cisco IOS has proven vulnerable to buffer overflows and other problems that have afflicted other operating systems and applications.

Note: Cisco recommends that all Cisco IOS devices implement the authentication, authorization, and accounting (AAA) security model. AAA can use local, RADIUS, and TACACS+ databases. However, a local account is usually still required for emergency situations.

See also

- NX-OS formerly known as SAN-OS
- Network operating system
- IOS XR
- JUNOS
- Supervisor Engine (Cisco)

External links

- Cisco Security Advisories; Complete History [4]
- Cisco IOS Commands [5]
- Cisco-centric Open Source Community [6]
- NMIS - Network Management Information System [7]
- Cisco 7200/3600 Simulator using IOS Images [8]
- Cisco IOS Packaging [9]
- Cisco IOS Internals [10]
- Rootkits on Cisco IOS Devices [11]
- Cisco Certification Forums [12]

PE router

PE router

Provider Edge router (**PE router**) is a router between one network service provider's area and areas administered by other network providers. A network provider is usually an Internet Service Provider as well (or only that).

The term *PE router* covers equipment capable of a broad range of routing protocols, notably:

- Border Gateway Protocol (BGP)
- Open Shortest Path First (OSPF)
- Multi-Protocol Label Switching (MPLS)

PE routers need not be aware of what kind of traffic is coming from the provider's network. However, some PE routers also do labeling.

See also

- CE router

Netgear

Netgear

NETGEAR®	
Type	Public (NASDAQ: NTGR [1])
Industry	Communications equipment
Founded	1996
Headquarters	San Jose, California
Key people	Patrick Lo, CEO & Chairman
Products	Hubs, Routers, DSL/Cable Gateways, Switches, Wireless Access Points, and Storage
Revenue	▲ US$743 million (2008)
Employees	565 (Q2 2009)
Website	http://www.netgear.com

NETGEAR, founded in 1996, is a US manufacturer of computer networking equipment and other computer hardware.

The company was incorporated January 8, 1996 as a subsidiary of Bay Networks, to "focus on providing networking solutions for small businesses and homes." In August 1998, the company was purchased by Nortel as part of its acquisition of Bay Networks. NETGEAR remained a wholly owned subsidiary of Nortel until March 2000, when it began transitioning to third-party ownership. It became fully independent from Nortel as of February 2002.

Netgear sells primarily through a sales channel network, which includes traditional retailers, online retailers, direct market resellers, value added resellers, and broadband service providers in North America, Europe, Middle East, Africa, and Asia Pacific. Its main retail competitors are Linksys and D-Link. In 2007, the United States (38% of revenue) and the United Kingdom (52%) were the company's two largest markets; however, EMEA and Asia Pacific were the fastest growing, with growth rates of 28% and 34%, respectively.

Product Range

Netgear's range of products are primarily focused in the networking market, with networking products for home and business use, including wired and wireless technology.

Netgear ADSL router

ProSafe Switches

Netgear markets a range of network products for the business sector, most notably their ProSafe switch range. As of May 2007, Netgear provide limited lifetime warranties across their entire range of ProSafe products for as long as the original buyer owns the product..

8 Port Gigabit Switch GS108

Network Appliances

Netgear also markets various network appliances for the business sector, such as managed switches and wired and wireless VPN firewalls. The firewalls compete in the SoHo and SMB market with Linksys, as well as with software distributions such as pfSense, m0n0wall, SmoothWall, and Untangle. The managed switches compete with HP ProCurve Networking and 3Com.

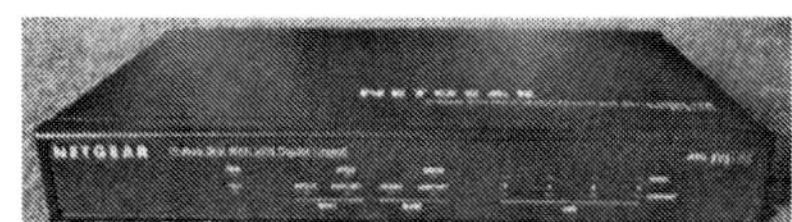

Dual WAN Gigabit VPN Firewall FVS336G

Security Appliances

2009 Netgear launched the ProSecure product range with all-in-one gateway solutions for small businesses and branch-offices(UTM series) and stream-scanning-appliances for 100-600 concurrent users. They use the Stream-Scanning technologies by CP-Secure. In combination with the managed layer 3 switches and professional NAS devices in 19", Netgear addresses value added resellers new security resellers.

Network Attached Storage

Netgear sells a line of premium NAS devices to small businesses and consumers under the product name ReadyNAS. With this storage hardware line, Netgear vies with competitors like Buffalo and HP to deliver NAS solutions to target market segments. Netgear entered the storage market in May of 2007 when it acquired Infrant (originator of the ReadyNAS line). In March of 2009, Netgear began to offer an integrated online backup solution called the ReadyNAS Vault. In November 2009, Netgear upgraded its iSCSI SAN target to LIO [2].

Manufacturing

Netgear outsources some of its manufacturing to other electronics companies, including Askey Computer Corporation, Asus, Cameo Communications, Delta Networks, Foxconn, Senao and SerComm. Netgear believes by outsourcing its manufacturing means it is able to deliver a better cost price to consumers as well as keeping the quality to their expected standard.

Quality

Some internet enthusiast sites reported buggy products in consumer wireless routers during 2003. For example, there was a class action lawsuit against the Netgear WGT624, claiming it contained faulty hardware or firmware.[12]

Notable products

Platinum II Enclosure

NETGEAR's Platinum II Enclosure (a case design used in most of NETGEAR's consumer products) was winner of a 2004 Good Design Award from the Chicago Athenaeum [3], created in conjunction with NewDealDesign.

See also

- WGR614L
- WNR3500L
- Netgear SC101
- Netgear DG834G
- Netgear FVS336G

External links

- Official website [4]
- Netgear profile on Wikinvest
- Netgear DSL router resource [5]]
- Netgear ProSafe GS110TP Switch Review V3.co.uk [6]
- Netgear Readynas Ultra 4 Review TheInquirer.net [7]

Gateway (telecommunications)

Gateway (telecommunications)

In telecommunications, the term **gateway** has the following meaning:

Juniper SRX210 service gateway

- In a communications network, a network node equipped for interfacing with another network that uses different protocols.
  - A gateway may contain devices such as protocol translators, impedance matching devices, rate converters, fault isolators, or signal translators as necessary to provide systeminteroperability. It also requires the establishment of mutually acceptable administrative procedures between both networks.
  - A protocol translation/mapping gateway interconnects networks with different network protocol technologies by performing the required protocol conversions.
- Loosely, a computer configured to perform the tasks of a gateway. For a specific case, see default gateway.

Routers exemplify special cases of gateways.

Gateways, also called **protocol converters**, can operate at any layer of the OSI model. The job of a gateway is much more complex than that of a router or switch. Typically, a gateway must convert one protocol stack into another.

Details

A gateway is a network point that acts as an entrance to another network. On the Internet, a node or stopping point can be either a gateway node or a host (end-point) node. Both the computers of Internet users and the computers that serve pages to users are host nodes, while the nodes that connect the networks in between are gateways. For example, the computers that control traffic between company networks or the computers used by internet service providers (ISPs) to connect users to the internet are gateway nodes.

In the network for an enterprise, a computer server acting as a gateway node is often also acting as a proxy server and a firewall server. A gateway is often associated with both a router, which knows where to direct a given packet of data that arrives at the gateway, and a switch, which furnishes the actual path in and out of the gateway for a given packet.

On an IP network, clients should automatically send IP packets with a destination outside a given subnet mask to a network gateway. A subnet mask defines the IP range of a network. For example, if a network has a base IP address of 192.168.0.0 and has a subnet mask of 255.255.255.0, then any data going to an IP address outside of 192.168.0.X will be sent to that network's gateway. While forwarding an IP packet to another network, the gateway might or might not perform Network Address Translation.

A gateway is an essential feature of most routers, although other devices (such as any PC or server) can function as a gateway.

Most computer operating systems use the terms described above. A computer running Microsoft Windows however describes this standard networking feature as Internet Connection Sharing; which will act as a gateway, offering a connection between the Internet and an internal network. Such a system might also act as a DHCP server. Dynamic Host Configuration Protocol (DHCP) is a protocol used by networked devices (clients) to obtain various parameters necessary for the clients to operate in an Internet Protocol (IP) network. By using this protocol, system administration workload greatly decreases, and devices can be added to the network with minimal or no manual configurations.

Internet-to-Orbit Gateway

An Internet to orbit gateway (I2O) is a machine that acts as a connector between computers or devices connected to the Internet and computer systems orbiting the earth, like satellites or even manned spacecrafts. Such connection is made when the I2O establishes a stable link between the spacecraft and a computer or a network of computers on the Internet, such link can be control signals, audio frequency, or even visible spectrum signals.

Project HERMES is the first of this kind of devices to become operative. The HERMES-A/MINOTAUR Space Flight Control Center became operative on June 6 2009 and was operated by representatives of 34 countries on the UNOOSA Symposium of Small Satellites for Sustainable Development in Graz, Austria on September 10, 2009. Project HERMES is an initiative of the Ecuadorian Civilian Space Agency and has a maximum coverage of 22,000 km, HERMES-A is supposed to be the first gateway of a network of five covering all south America. HERMES-A/MINOTAUR is not only capable of data transmission but voice also.

Project GENSO is an initiative from NASA and ESA, and it is expected to begin operations on April 2010, it is supposed to have worldwide coverage

Examples

- A very popular example is connecting a Local Area Network or Wireless LAN to the Internet or other Wide Area Network. In this case the gateway connects a LAN to the provider-specific network which in turn connects to the Internet. In the case of a home, this gateway is called a residential gateway.
- MainWay is the Bull brand for a gateway which connects DSA to TCP/IP

Sources

- Federal Standard 1037C
- MIL-STD-188

See also

- Router
- Subnet

Wireless Router Application Platform

Wireless Router Application Platform

The **Wireless Router Application Platform** (**WRAP**) is a format of single board computer defined by Swiss company PC Engines. This is specially designed for wireless router, firewall, load balancer, VPN or other network appliances.

Basic specs

- 32-bit x86 compatible CPU, low energy consumption (AMD Geode SC1100 at 266 MHz)
- supports MMX instructions
- 64-bit SDRAM memory controller (max: 89 MHz)
- PCI bus controller
- IDE interfaces
- ACPI 1.0-compatible power management
- tinyBIOS : Made specially by PC Engines
- 64 or 128MB SDRAM
- Compact flash memory (includes boot OS)
- Monitoring: watchdog timer, LM77 thermal monitor
- Power supply: 7V ~ 18V external DC power or Power over Ethernet
- LAN: National semiconductor DP83816
- I/O: MiniPCI slots, console serial port

Different boards

There are three different models of the WRAP:

- The WRAP 1-1 has two Ethernet ports, and two mini-PCI slots, on a 16x16cm board.
- The WRAP 1-2 has three Ethernet ports and one mini-PCI slot, on a 16x16cm board.
- The WRAP 2 has one Ethernet port, and two mini-PCI slots, on a 10x16cm board.

Operating System

The WRAP is capable of running many different operating systems, including various Linux distributions, FreeBSD, NetBSD, OpenBSD, as well as proprietary OSes. The WRAP lacks a keyboard controller (for obvious reasons), so some OSes that rely on one for the boot process may have to be modified.

End Of Life (EOL)

PC Engines announced the end of life for the WRAP platform in 2007. The board was replaced by the ALIX.

External links

- PC Engines information page on the WRAP [1]
- BowlFish [2]

Cellular router

Cellular router

Cellular routers are routers that provide shared Internet access by incorporating a cellular data modem and providing traditional interfaces like Ethernet and WiFi.

They can be deployed as a primary WAN link to a location where wired connections are not cost-effective, can also be used as a secondary or business continuity plan should the primary cabled link fail, or can be used in moving vehicles to provide Internet access while in motion. Cellular routers range from simple SOHO network oriented devices through rugged industrial units with advanced features.

Types

There are two types:

- Compact: the cellular modem and the router are the same device. These are also called "integrated" or "embedded" cellular routers.
- Modular: one can connect the cellular modem to the router. These are sometimes called "slide" devices if there is a receptacle for a cellular data card. Other types allow for a USB wireless modem to plug in.

Vyatta

Vyatta

Type	Private
Industry	LAN, Wide area network, Security appliance, Internet security, Network security
Founded	2005
Headquarters	Belmont, CA
Key people	CEO: Kelly Herrell
Products	Router, Firewall, VPN, SSL VPN, Intrusion prevention, DHCP, Network Address Translation URL Filtering Web Caching Network Virtualization
Employees	25-50
Website	http://www.vyatta.com

Vyatta manufactures an open source router/firewall/VPN product for Internet Protocol networks (IPv4 and IPv6). A free download of Vyatta has been available since March 2006. The system is a specialized Debian-based Linux distribution with networking applications such as Quagga, OpenVPN, and many others. A standardized management console, similar to Juniper JUNOS or Cisco IOS, in addition to a web-based GUI and traditional Linux system commands, provides configuration of the system and applications.

Vyatta is also delivered as virtual machines to offer virtual networking (vrouter, vfirewall, VPN) functionality for Xen, VMware, Hyper-V and Amazon EC2 virtual and cloud computing environments.

Commercial engagements are available via integrated hardware appliances and a subscription-based business model which includes software updates, technical support, and training. Vyatta also offers a series of professional services and consulting engagements.

The Vyatta system is intended as a replacement for Cisco IOS 1800 through ASR 1000 series Integrated Services Routers (ISR) and ASA 5500 security appliances, with a strong emphasis on the cost and flexibility inherent in an open source, Linux-based system running on commodity x86 hardware or in Xen or VMware virtual environments. Vyatta also provides a Cisco Replacement Guide on its website which shows various Cisco products and the comparable Vyatta/x86 solutions.

External links

- Vyatta Website [1]
- Vyatta Community Website [2]
- Vyatta Virtualization site [3]
- Intel Performance Benchmark using Vyatta [4]
- Vyatta vs. Cisco 7204 Performance Test [5]

Router clustering

Router clustering

A patented technology of FatPipe Networks, "**router clustering**" to define aggregating of multiple, disparate routers into one device.

Router Cluster

Two or more routers grouped together to provide any combination of hardware redundancy, service redundancy, load balancing and increased speed. The speed enhancement is accomplished by aggregating the routers together. For example, three separate routers such as T1, T3, E1, E3 or wireless can be combined to provide three times the speed, reliability and redundancy. Although failover can be accomplished in routers through software, all of the features mentioned above either require additional hardware within the router or an external router cluster device.

More information is available in U.S. Patent 6493341 [1]

Passport Carrier Release

Passport Carrier Release

Passport Carrier Release (PCR) is a version of the Passport Switch (now Multiservice Switch) software designed to run in telecommunications carrier environments. It was formerly developed by Nortel. After the sale in 2009 of most Nortel's assets, the passport SW is still used in several products of Alcatel-Lucent, Ericsson and Kapsch.

Technologies

Internally, PCR is largely built up of custom applications on top of a VxWorks kernel. A benefit of the software is that it is completely modular and can load components to Passport control processors (CPs) and function processors (FPs) on an as-needed basis. FPs (also known as line cards) each run their own instance of the Operating System, and as such can be rebooted without the need to take the entire switch out of service, for example due to a software failure. As well, as would be expected, entire cards can be replaced while the system is hot, thus minimizing downtime due to hardware failure.

OAM and Provisioning

PCR consists of a custom OAM interface that is highly object oriented. This reflects the modular nature of the operating system. The core component when provisioning IP networks is the Virtual Router (however, a Passport switch can act in more than IP environments). Interfaces are provisioned as "application" objects, which are then in turn connected to Protocol Ports on a Virtual Router. It is best to consider the environment in which provisioning occurs to be object oriented, in the sense that the behaviour of the router is defined based on which objects are instantiated and how they are related. Note that there is a change in this paradigm noticeable in recent releases of PCR -- MPLS, for example, now resides on an object called simply a Router with built-in IP features. This provisioning approach is more similar to that of Cisco or Juniper Networks.

Drawbacks

Unfortunately, at this time the OAM interface is unable to select which components are to be loaded on the fly. For example, if Multi-link Point-to-Point Protocol (PPP) is a required feature, before this feature can be used the CP and the FP hosting the MLPPP interface must have the mlppp feature loaded. As well, the vast array of objects available to an operator can be daunting, especially for an individual starting out with Nortel Passport switches for the first time. As well, built in documentation leaves much to be desired (thus not helping the first-time operator), and tab completion features are non-existent (though some objects and parameters have shorthand names, for example the Virtual Router component can simply be known as a Vr).

Versioning

PCR releases are assigned a release code, usually of the form CG##X, where ## is a two digit number and X is a letter, usually referring to a patch code or revision code.

The current release is PCR 9.1.1.

See also

- Nortel
- List of Nortel Products and Protocols
- Multiservice Switch

External links

- Nortel Multiservice Switch Portfolio [1]
- Nortel Corporate Website [2]
- Sample of how to configure SNMP on PCR (for use with MRTG) [3]

Core router

Core router

This article is about a computer router used on the Internet backbone. For the kind used within a network, see Router. For other types see: Core router (disambiguation).

A **core router** is a router designed to operate in the Internet backbone, or core. To fulfill this role, a router must be able to support multiple telecommunications interfaces of the highest speed in use in the core Internet and must be able to forward IP packets at full speed on all of them. It must also support the routing protocols being used in the core. A core router is distinct from an edge router: edge routers sit at the edge of a backbone network and connect to core routers.

Cisco CRS-1 Backbone Core Router

History

Like the term "supercomputer", the term "core router" refers to the largest and most capable routers of the then-current generation. A router that was a core router when introduced will not be a core router ten years later. At the inception of the ARPANET (the Internet's predecessor) in 1969, the fastest links were 56 kbit/s and a given routing node had at most six links. The "core router" was a dedicated minicomputer called an IMP Interface Message Processor. Link speeds increased steadily, requiring progressively more powerful routers until the mid-1990s, when the typical core link speed reached 155 Mbit/s. At that time, several breakthroughs in fiber optic telecommunications (notably DWDM and EDFA) technologies combined to permit a sudden dramatic increase in core link speeds: by 2000, a core link operated at 2.5 Gbit/s and core internet companies were planning for 10 Gbit/s speeds.

The Internet was historically supply-limited, and core Internet providers historically struggled to expand the Internet to meet the demand. During the late 1990s, they expected a radical increase in demand, driven by the Dot-com bubble. By 2001, it became apparent that the sudden expansion in core link capacity had outstripped the actual demand for internet services in the core. The core internet providers were able to defer purchases of new core routers for a time, and most of the new companies went out of business. Cisco and Juniper were able to deliver their newest core router products several years later.

As of 2007, the internet core link speed is 10 Gbit/s, with a few links at 40 Gbit/s. Cisco's core router is the CRS-1 and Juniper's core routers comprise the T-series.

Core router manufacturers

(core router model between parenthesis)

- Brocade Communications Systems (NetIron XMR Series)
- Cisco Systems (CRS series)
- Extreme Networks (Black Diamond 20808), high-end core switch
- Huawei Technologies Ltd. (NetEngine 5000E, NetEngine 80E, NetEngine 80)
- Juniper Networks (T-series)
- Nortel Networks (Secure Router 8000 Series), small-scale core routers only
- ZTE (ZXR10 Series : T8000,M6000)

Failed core router companies

- Axiowave Networks
- Allegro Networks
- Avici Systems (changed name to Soapstone Networks in 2008 and no longer making core routers)
- Caspian Networks
- Charlotte's Web Networks
- Foundry Networks (acquired by Brocade in 2008)
- Hyperchip
- IPOptical
- Ironbridge
- Marconi (still in business, not making core routers)
- Osphere Net Systems
- Pluris
- Procket Networks (acquired by Cisco Systems in 2004)

See also

- Cisco Systems acquisitions

WAAV, Inc.

WAAV, Inc.

Type	Private
Industry	Network hardware manufacturing
Founded	2004
Founder(s)	J.C. Fulknier
Headquarters	Cambridge, Massachusetts, United States
Key people	President: Brian J. Smith
Products	Network hardware for mobile Wi-Fi hotspots (in vehicles)

WAAV, Inc., formerly Omniwav Mobile, Inc., offers mobile Wi-Fi routers and solutions designed for high-quality signal delivery and reliable performance. The company manufactures and sells mobile broadband cellular routers using the most advanced networks. Waav was founded by a group of Computer network, Telecom, and Radio frequency (RF) engineers in San Diego, CA in 2004. Since then, the company has pioneered mobile cellular equipment for custom car clients such as Snoop Dogg and corporate fleets including Bolt Bus (Greyhound) and Peter Pan Bus Lines. In 2008, Waav wired the commuter rail division of Boston's mass transit agency, the Massachusetts Bay Transportation Authority (MBTA), making it the first US rail carrier to offer Wi-Fi service. Other deployments have involved custom cars, first-responder police/fire vehicles and the train used by U.S. President Barack Obama during his January 2009 inaugural trip to Washington DC.

WAAV (pronounced "Wave") has been featured in Business 2.0, Entrepreneur Magazine, and others business outlets. The company is privately held and has its corporate headquarters in Cambridge, MA.

Routing control plane

Routing control plane

In **routing**, the **control plane** is the part of the router architecture that is concerned with drawing the network map, or the information in a (possibly augmented) routing table that defines what to do with incoming packets. Control plane functions, such as participating in routing protocols, run in the architectural control element. In most cases, the routing table contains a list of destination addresses and the outgoing interface(s) associated with them. Control plane logic also can define certain packets to be discarded, as well as preferential treatment of certain packets for which a high quality of service is defined by such mechanisms as differentiated services.

Depending on the specific router implementation, there may be a separate forwarding information base that is populated (i.e., loaded) by the Control Plane, but used by the forwarding plane to look up packets, at very high speed, and decide how to handle them.

Building the unicast routing table

A major function of the control plane is deciding which routes go into the main routing table. "Main" refers to the table that holds the unicast routes that are active. multicast routing may require an additional routing table for multicast routes. Several routing protocols e.g. OSPF and BGP maintain internal data bases of candidate routes which are promoted when a route fails or when a routing policy is changed.

Several different information sources may provide information about a route to a given destination, but the router must select the "best" route to install into the routing table. In some cases, there may be multiple routes of equal "quality", and the router may install all of them and load-share across them.

Sources of routing information

There are three general sources of routing information:

- Information on the status of directly connected hardware and software-defined interfaces
- Manually configured static routes
- Information from (dynamic) routing protocols

Local interface information

Routers forward traffic that enters on an input interface and leaves on an output interface, subject to filtering and other local rules. While routers usually forward from one physical (e.g., Ethernet, serial) to another physical interface, it is also possible to define multiple logical interfaces on a physical interface. A physical Ethernet interface, for example, can have logical interfaces in several virtual LANs defined by IEEE 802.1Q VLAN headers.

When an interface has an address configured in a subnet, such as 192.0.2.1 in the 192.0.2.0/24 (i.e., subnet mask 255.255.255.0) subnet, and that interface is considered "up" by the router, the router thus has a directly connected route to 192.0.2.0/24. If a routing protocol offered another router's route to that same subnet, the routing table installation software will normally ignore the dynamic route and prefer the directly connected route.

There also may be software-only interfaces on the router, which it treats as if they were locally connected. For example, most implementations have a "null" software-defined interface. Packets having this interface as a next hop will be discarded, which can be a very efficient way to filter traffic. Routers usually can route traffic faster than they can examine it and compare it to filters, so, if the criterion for discarding is the packet's destination address, "blackholing" the traffic will be more efficient than explicit filters.

Other software defined interfaces that are treated as directly connected, as long as they are active, are interfaces associated with tunneling protocols such as generic routing encapsulation (GRE) or Multi-Protocol Label Switching (MPLS).

Static routes

Router configuration rules may contain static routes. A static route minimally has a destination address, a prefix length or subnet mask, and a definition where to send packets for the route. That definition can refer to a local interface on the router, or a next-hop address that could be on the far end of a subnet to which the router is connected. The next-hop address could also be on a subnet that is directly connected, and, before the router can determine if the static route is usable, it must do a **recursive lookup** of the next hop address in the local routing table. If the next-hop address is reachable, the static route is usable, but if the next-hop is unreachable, the route is ignored.

Static routes also may have preference factors used to select the best static route to the same destination. One application is called a **floating static route**, where the static route is less preferred than a route from any routing protocol. The static route, which might use a dialup link or other slow medium, activates only when the dynamic routing protocol(s) cannot provide a route to the destination.

Static routes that are more preferred than any dynamic route also can be very useful, especially when using traffic engineering principles to make certain traffic go over a specific path with an engineered quality of service.

Dynamic routing protocols

See routing protocols. The routing table manager, according to implementation and configuration rules, may select a particular route or routes from those advertised by various routing protocols.

Installing unicast routes

Different implementations have different sets of preferences for routing information, and these are not standardized among IP routers. It is fair to say that subnets on directly connected active interfaces are always preferred. Beyond that, however, there will be differences.

Implementers generally have a numerical preference, which Cisco calls an "administrative distance", for route selection. The lower the preference, the more desirable the route. Cisco's IOS implementation makes exterior BGP the most preferred source of dynamic routing information, while Nortel RS makes intra-area OSPF most preferred.

The general order of selecting routes to install is:

1. If the route is not in the routing table, install it.
2. If the route is "more specific" than an existing route, install it in addition to the existing routes. "More specific" means that it has a longer prefix. A /28 route, with a subnet mask of 255.255.255.240, is more specific than a /24 route, with a subnet mask of 255.255.255.0.
3. If the route is of equal specificity to a route already in the routing table, but comes from a more preferred source of routing information, replace the route in the table.
4. If the route is of equal specificity to a route in the routing table, comes from a source of the same preference,
   1. Discard it if the route has a higher metric than the existing route
   2. Replace the existing route if the new route has a lower metric
   3. If the routes are of equal metric and the router supports load-sharing, add the new route and designate it as part of a load-sharing group. Typically, implementations will support a maximum number of routes that load-share to the same destination. If that maximum is already in the table, the new route is usually dropped.

Relationship between the routing table and forwarding information base

See forwarding plane for more detail, but each implementation has its own means of updating the forwarding information base with new routes installed in the routing table. If the FIB is in one-to-one correspondence with the RIB, the new route is installed in the FIB after it is in the RIB. If the FIB is smaller than the RIB, and the FIB uses a hash table or other data structure that does not easily update, the existing FIB might be invalidated and replaced with a new one computed from the updated RIB.

Multicast routing tables

Multicast routing builds on unicast routing. Each multicast group to which the local router can route has a multicast routing table entry with a next hop for the group, rather than for a specific destination as in unicast routing.

There can be multicast static routes as well as learning dynamic multicast routes from a protocol such as Protocol Independent Multicast (PIM).

Forwarding plane

Forwarding plane

In routing, the **forwarding plane**, sometimes called the **data plane**, defines the part of the router architecture that decides what to do with packets arriving on an inbound interface. Most commonly, it refers to a table in which the router looks up the destination address of the incoming packet and retrieves the information necessary to determine the path from the receiving element, through the internal **forwarding fabric** of the router, and to the proper outgoing interface(s). The IP Multimedia Subsystem architecture uses the term **transport plane** to describe a function roughly equivalent to the routing control plane.

Cisco VIP 2-40, from an older generation of routers.

The table also might specify that the packet is discarded. In some cases, the router will return an ICMP "destination unreachable" or other appropriate code. Some security policies, however, dictate that the router should be programmed to drop the packet silently. By dropping filtered packets silently, a potential attacker does not become aware of a target that is being protected.

Performance Route Processor, from the high-end Cisco 12000 series.

The incoming forwarding element will also decrement the time-to-live (TTL) field of the packet, and, if the new value is zero, discard the packet. While the Internet Protocol (IP) specification indicates that an Internet Control Message Protocol (ICMP) "TTL exceeded" message should be sent to the originator of the packet (i.e., the node with the source address in the packet), routers may be programmed to drop the packet silently.

Depending on the specific router implementation, the table in which the destination address is looked up could be the routing table (also known as the routing information base, RIB), or a separate forwarding information base (FIB) that is populated (i.e., loaded) by the routing control plane, but used by the forwarding plane to look up packets, at very high speed, and decide how to handle them. Before or after examining the destination, other tables may be consulted to make decisions to drop the packet based on other characteristics, such as the source address, the IP protocol identifier field, or

Transmission Control Protocol (TCP) or User Datagram Protocol (UDP) port number.

Forwarding plane functions run in the forwarding element. . High-performance routers often have multiple distributed forwarding elements, so that the router increases performance with parallel processing.

The outgoing interface will encapsulate the packet in the appropriate data link protocol. Depending on the router software and its configuration, functions, usually implemented at the outgoing interface, may set various packet fields, such as the DSCP field used by differentiated services.

In general, the passage from the input interface directly to an output interface, through the fabric with minimum modification at the output interface, is called the *fast path* of the router. If the packet needs significant processing, such as segmentation or encryption, it may go onto a slower path, which is sometimes called the *services plane* of the router. Service planes can make forwarding or processing decisions based on higher-layer information, such as a Web URL contained in the packet payload.

Issues in router forwarding performance

Vendors design router products for specific markets. Design of routers intended for home use, perhaps supporting several PCs and VoIP telephony, is driven by keeping the cost as low as possible. In such a router, there is no separate forwarding fabric, and there is only one active forwarding path: into the main processor and out of the main processor.

Routers for more demanding applications accept greater cost and complexity to get higher throughput in their forwarding planes.

Several design factors affect router forwarding performance:

- Data link layer processing and extracting the packet
- Decoding the packet header
- Looking up the destination address in the packet header
- Analyzing other fields in the packet
- Sending the packet through the "fabric" interconnecting the ingress and egress interfaces
- Processing and data link encapsulation at the egress interface

Routers may have one or more processors. In a uniprocessor design, these performance parameters are affected not just by the processor speed, but by competition for the processor. Higher-performance routers invariably have multiple processing elements, which may be general-purpose processor chips or specialized application-specific integrated circuits (ASIC).

Very high performance products have multiple processing elements on each interface card. In such designs, the main processor does not participate in forwarding, but only in control plane and management processing.

Benchmarking performance

In the Internet Engineering Task Force, two working groups in the Operations & Maintenance Area deal with aspects of performance. The Interprovider Performance Measurement (IPPM) group focuses, as its name would suggest, on operational measurement of services. Performance measurements on single routers, or narrowly defined systems of routers, are the province of the Benchmarking Working Group (BMWG).

RFC 2544 is the key BMWG document . A classic RFC 2544 benchmark uses half the router's (i.e., the device under test (DUT)) ports for input of a defined load, and measures the time at which the outputs appear at the output ports.

Forwarding information base design

Originally, all destinations were looked up in the RIB. Perhaps the first step in speeding routers was to have a separate RIB and FIB in main memory, with the FIB, typically with fewer entries than the RIB, being organized for fast destination lookup. In contrast, the RIB was optimized for efficient updating by routing protocols.

Early uniprocessing routers usually organized the FIB as a hash table, while the RIB might be a linked list. Depending on the implementation, the FIB might have fewer entries than the RIB, or the same number.

When routers started to have separate forwarding processors, these processors usually had far less memory than the main processor, such that the forwarding processor could hold only the most frequently used routes. On the early Cisco AGS+ and 7000, for example, the forwarding processor cache could hold approximately 1000 route entries. In an enterprise, this would often work quite well, because there were fewer than 1000 server or other popular destination subnets. Such a cache, however, was far too small for general Internet routing. Different router designs behaved in different ways when a destination was not in the cache.

Cache miss issues

A **cache miss** condition might result in the packet being sent back to the main processor, to be looked up in a **slow path** that had access to the full routing table. Depending on the router design, a cache miss might cause an update to the fast hardware cache or the fast cache in main memory. In some designs, it was most efficient to invalidate the fast cache for a cache miss, send the packet that caused the cache miss through the main processor, and then repopulate the cache with a new table that included the destination that caused the miss. This approach is similar to an operating system with virtual memory, which keeps the most recently used information in physical memory.

As memory costs went down and performance needs went up, FIBs emerged that had the same number of route entries as in the RIB, but arranged for fast lookup rather than fast update. Whenever a RIB entry changed, the router changed the corresponding FIB entry.

FIB design alternatives

High-performance FIBs achieve their speed with implementation-specific combinations of specialized algorithms and hardware.

Software

Various search algorithms have been used for FIB lookup. While well-known general-purpose data structures were first used, such as hash tables, specialized algorithms, optimized for IP addresses, emerged. They include:

- Binary tree
- Radix tree
- Four-way trie
- Patricia tree

Since 2006, multicore CPU is changing the design of Fast Path thanks to innovative processors such as the Cavium's Octeon, RMI's XLS/XLR/XLP, Freescale's QorIQ or even using Intel's multicore processors. Now, it is based on dedicated data path software into the cores of those CPUs. The coding rules of software have changed. The system has to be made of a dedicated packet engine stack on each core, which cannot be a regular OS stack; each instance is spread into the cluster of cores in order to be the Fast Path. Into this Fast Path, since it runs in a highly parallel system, in order to achieve the highest performance of a data plane, only lock free algorithms are allowed.

Hardware

Various forms of fast RAM and, eventually, basic content addressable memory (CAM) were used to speed lookup. CAM, while useful in layer 2 switches that needed to look up a relatively small number of fixed-length MAC addresses, had limited utility with IP addresses having variable-length routing prefixes (see Classless Inter-Domain Routing). Ternary CAM (CAM), while expensive, lends itself to variable-length prefix lookups .

One of the challenges of forwarder lookup design is to minimize the amount of specialized memory needed, and, increasingly, to minimize the power consumed by memory.

Distributed forwarding

A next step in speeding routers was to have a specialized forwarding processor separate from the main processor. There was still a single path, but forwarding no longer had to compete with control in a single processor. The fast routing processor typically had a small FIB, with hardware memory (e.g., static random access memory (SRAM)) faster and more expensive than the FIB in main memory. Main memory was generally dynamic random access memory (DRAM).

Early distributed forwarding

Next, routers began to have multiple forwarding elements, that communicated through a high-speed **shared bus** or through a **shared memory**. Cisco used shared busses until they saturated, while Juniper preferred shared memory .

Each forwarding element had its own FIB. See, for example, the Versatile Interface Processor on the Cisco 7500

Eventually, the shared resource became a bottleneck, with the limit of shared bus speed being roughly 2 million packets per second (Mpps). Crossbar fabrics broke through this bottleneck.

Shared paths become bottlenecks

As forwarding bandwidth increased, even with the elimination of cache miss overhead, the shared paths limited throughput. While a router might have 16 forwarding engines, if there was a single bus, only one packet transfer at a time was possible. There were some special cases where a forwarding engine might find that the output interface was one of the logical or physical interfaces present on the forwarder card, such that the packet flow was totally inside the forwarder. It was often easier, however, even in this special case, to send the packet out the bus and receive it from the bus.

While some designs experimented with multiple shared buses, the eventual approach was to adapt the crossbar switch model from telephone switches, in which every forwarding engine had a hardware path to every other forwarding engine. With a small number of forwarding engines, crossbar forwarding fabrics are practical and efficient for high-performance routing. There are multistage designs for crossbar systems, such as Clos networks.

See also

- Network processor
- Network Search Engine

Turing switch

Turing switch

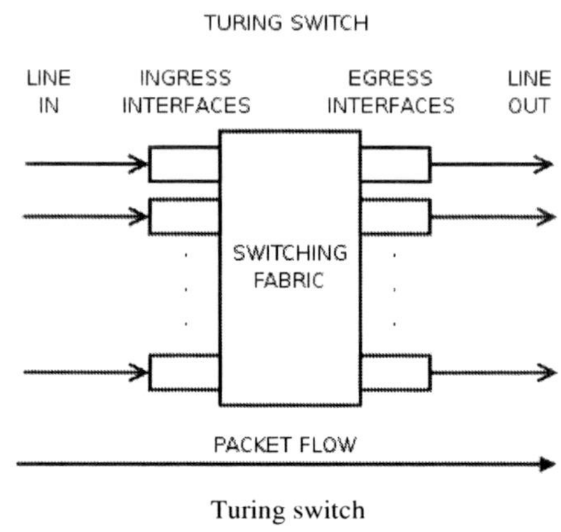

Turing switch

The **Turing switch** is a logical construction similar to the Turing machine. The Turing switch models the operation of a basic network switch in a network of switches, much the same as a Turing machine models the operation of a basic computational entity. Both are named in honor of the English logician Alan Turing. Some introductory research on the Turing switch was started at the University of Cambridge by Jon Crowcroft [1].

In essence, Crowcroft suggests that instead of using general purpose computers to do packet switching, the required operations should be reduced to application specific logic and then that application specific logic should be implemented using optical components. The work is not actually based on Turing's research.

A Turing switch consists of a switching fabric, one or more ingress interfaces (also referred to as sources), one or more egress interfaces (sinks), and a decision procedure to determine an egress interface given an ingress interface. Interfaces are sometimes referred to as ports. A packet (cell or switched unit) arrives at an ingress interface, the appropriate egress interface is determined by the decision procedure, and the packet is then transported across the switching fabric to the egress interface. A packet is a symbol or sequence of 1's and 0's. An ingress interface is connected to an ingress line, an egress interface to an egress line. The ingress line is said to feed the ingress interface; the egress interface feeds the egress line.

See also

- Network switch

Nexus Hawk

Nexus Hawk

The Nexus Hawk is a gateway router linking broadband cellular data, such as CDMA, GSM and Wi-Fi (IEEE 802.11a, b, g) and WAN (such as BGAN Satellite) networks providing enterprises with broadband wireless internet/network data services in mobile and remote environments.

The Nexus Hawk's original development was funded under a DOD prime contract. The technology was primarily designed for military use and supports public safety. The Nexus Hawk is currently in use by law enforcement agencies, governmental data infrastructure, commercial fleet, connectivity in and to retail locations, and livery services in Washington DC.

The device provides; secure access to public and private wired and wireless networks including; Sprint Nextel (CDMA EVDO Rev A, 1xRTT, Verizon Wireless CDMA EVDO Rev A 1xRTT, AT&T Wireless GSM /HSDPA, Telus CDMA EVDO Rev A 1xRTT, Washington DC EVDO Rev A Regional Wireless Broadband Network (RWBN), non-U.S. cellular networks, and secure WiFi. GPS for applications such as Automatic Vehicle Location (AVL) sometimes commercial referred to as fleet tracking or Geo-Based Dispatch and Navigation. Connectivity to multiple simultaneous WAN paths with user-selectable order for failover and fail back. Access to 4 simultaneous WANS and GPS. Automatic and persistent network connections. Incorporates a PCMCIA CardBus slot to accommodate future networks such as WiMAX and Public Safety Band), accepts ExpressCard 34mm air cards, PCMCIA CardBus air cards and USB air cards, Secure Remote Configuration Management, Built in IPsec and OpenVPN and pass through security features, FIPS140-2 SSL Certified Module.

See also

- HSPA
- Huawei E220

External links

- Nexus Hawk Official website [1]

Gaming router

Gaming router

A **gaming router** is a router that is specifically designed to optimize network traffic generated by video games. Specifically, the router's built-in quality of service mechanism gives gaming packets priority over all other network traffic.

Untangle

Untangle

Type	Private
Industry	Security software, Security appliances, Internet security, Network security
Founded	2003
Headquarters	San Mateo, CA
Key people	CEO: Bob Walters Founder: John Irwin Founder: Dirk Morris
Products	Web content filtering, Anti-spam, Antivirus, Anti-phishing, Anti-spyware, Intrusion prevention, Firewall, OpenVPN, SSL VPN
Employees	17
Website	www.untangle.com [1]

Untangle is a privately held company based in San Mateo, CA, USA. The company provides an open source network gateway for small businesses, schools, and non-profit organizations. Untangle provides multiple gateway applications installed at the edge of a network.

History

Untangle was founded in 2003 as Metavize, Inc. by John Irwin and Dirk Morris. Metavize officially launched in 2005 at Demo@15!. In 2006, Metavize raised a $10.5M series-A venture funding round from CMEA Ventures and Rustic Canyon Partners, named Bob Walters as CEO, and renamed to Untangle, Inc. In 2007, Untangle released the Untangle Gateway Platform as open source under the GPLv2 license , and surpassed 100,000 users in 2,000 organizations. In June 2009, Untangle claimed over 1 million protected users. In October 2009, Untangle released Untangle 7.0 which included improvements to its reporting capabilities. In December 2009, Untangle released Untangle 7.1 which included improvements to its web filtering and policy management applications. In March 2010, Untangle released Untangle 7.2 which included its Captive Portal application.

Untangle released a free bookmark utility called SaveFace in May 2010, in response to continued loosening of default privacy settings in Facebook user accounts.

Awards and recognition

In August 2008, Untangle was named a winner in InfoWorld's Best of Open Source Software awards.

Products

Untangle applications include Anti-spam, Web Content Filtering, Antivirus, Anti-phishing, Anti-spyware, Intrusion prevention, Firewall, OpenVPN, SSL VPN, Router, Protocol Control, Attack Blocker, Reporting, Policy Manager, Kaspersky Virus Blocker , Commtouch Spam Booster, ESoft Web Filter, Directory Connector, Captive Portal, Ad Blocker, WAN Balancer, WAN Failover, and Branding Manager on the Untangle Gateway Platform.

External links

- Official company website [1]

Timos

Timos

No Logo	
OS family	Unknown
Working state	Current
Kernel type	Unknown
License	Proprietary

TiMOS is a proprietary operating system used on most recent Alcatel-Lucent service routers and switches. Originally developed by Timetra , a US based startup firm. (TimOS stands for Timetra Operating System). Timetra was bought out by Alcatel-Lucent in 2004 after a period of mutual engagement in projects. TimOS is used primarily on the Service Routers 7750 Service Switches 7450 and Service Aggregation Routers 7705.

It has some similarities to Cisco IOS however no emulator (such as Dynamips or Olive) is publicly available, and little is publicly known of the OS.

See also

- 5620 sam

Netgear FVS336G

Netgear FVS336G

The **Netgear ProSafe Dual WAN VPN Firewall FVS336G** is a network appliance by Netgear. It runs Linux and bootstraps with RedBoot. It has two gigabit Ethernet WAN ports capable of link aggregation. It has a 4-port gigabit Ethernet switch. It can host both IPsec and SSL VPN, supporting up to 25 simultaneous tunnels with IPsec or 10 with SSL. It supports dynamic DNS and a stateful packet inspection firewall. It has a built-in AC/DC power supply, only requiring a standard IEC power cable. It has a 300MHz processor and an internal JTAG interface. It supports QoS packet prioritization for both TCP and UDP. It does not currently support uPNP or NAT-PMP although this could change with future firmware updates; but it does support port triggering.

External links

- Netgear official page for FVS336G Wired VPN Firewall [1]
- Netgear FVS336G official firmware releases [2]
- SmallNetBuilder NETGEAR FVS336G Reviewed: VPN Your Way [3]

Junxion

Junxion

Junxion is a company known for its cellular routers in a recognizable lime green color. These network appliance products used embedded distribution of Linux (called Junxion OS) and contained a PCMCIA card slot for supplying the mobile wireless PC card.

Simply put, a Junxion Box uses the data plan of a mobile service card, such as EDGE or EVDO, and acts as a NAT router host for upstream bandwidth provision as a typical local area network using ethernet. These could also be used as a secondary fall-over provider with an existing dual-WAN router.

On 5 August 2008, the acquisition of Juxion by Sierra Wireless was announced.

See also

- Femtocell
- Fixed-mobile convergence
- Generic Access Network (GAN), also known as Unlicensed Mobile Access (UMA)

External links

- Junxion official site [1]
  - Junxion Box and OS [2]
  - Field Commander [3]
- BoingBoing: Verizon doesn't like Junxion boxes [4]
- ClNet Junxion Box review [5] includes video and panorama images of the device
- StompBox Networks [6] explains how WWAN routers are constructed

NetHope NetReliefKit

NetHope NetReliefKit

The **NetReliefKit** from NetHope is a solar powered wireless Internet router that provides data and voice connectivity via satellite in remote locations. Developed by Cisco and Inmarsat, the device was deployed to internet signals after the 2004 Indian Ocean earthquake.

Juniper M Series

Juniper M Series

M series family routers	
Date invented	1998
Manufacturer	Juniper Networks
Type	Network Router
Processor	Internet Processor

Juniper M Series is a series of Multiservice Edge routers designed and manufactured by Juniper Networks, for enterprise and service provider networks. It spans over M7i, M10i, M40e, M120, and M320 platforms with 7 Gbit/s up to 320 Gbit/s of throughput. The *M40* router was the first product by Juniper Networks, which was released in 1998. The M Series routers run on JUNOS Operating System.

Models and Platforms

M Series Platform of Juniper routers includes the models like M7i, M10i, M40e, M120, and M320 routers. M40 and M20 platform routers have reached the end of sale.

M40

M40 was the first product by Juniper Networks, which was released in 1998. The M40 was the first of its kind capable of scaling to meet the internet standards ,which can move 40 million packets per second with a throughput rate in excess of 40 gigabits per second. With the initial offering of m40, Juniper came up with the *Internet Processor I*. The proprietary ASIC was the fundamental core of Juniper's *Packet Forwarding Engine* (PFE). The PFE consisted of a shared memory, a single forwarding table, and a one-write, one-read architecture.The entire PFE was capable of forwarding at 40 Mpps, a capacity more than 100 times faster than that of any other available router architectures at that time. The M40 is one of the first routers on this scale, about 10 times faster than Cisco's 12000.

The M Series were also the first in the industry to offer a true decoupling of the Control Plane and the forwarding plane.

M20

M20 was the second router introduced by Juniper Networks which was released in December 1999. The M20 also uses the Internet Processor II ASIC and is capable of throughput in excess of 20Gbit/s.The M20 was the first Juniper router available with redundancy (power supply, routing engine, and system and switch board [SSB]).

M160

The M160 router which was introduced in March 2000 as the third box in the M Series from Juniper Networks. Independent testing has shown that the M160 outperforms the competition in areas of BGP table capacity, MPLS LSP capacity, route flapping recovery at OC-192 speeds, convergence at both OC-192 and OC-48 speeds, and filtering at both OC-192 and OC-48 speeds. In additional tests, the M160 has matched or exceeded the competition in the areas of CoS at OC-48 and OC-192 speeds and IP and MPLS baseline testing at OC-48 and OC-192 speeds.

M5 and M10

They were introduced at the same time in September 2000, because they had similar architectures with two different throughput capabilities (5 Gbit/s on the M5 and 10Gbit/s on the M10). Both routers employs the *Internet Processor II* ASIC, providing forwarding table lookups at 40Mpps.There are two forwarding engine boards (FEBs) in the M10, allowing for a maximum of eight physical interface cards (PICs) to be used.

M40e

The M40e platform was introduced in February 2002. The M40e router has the same port density as the M40, but it provides the optional redundancy that the M40 didn't have. This model is compatible with most of the PICs from the M20, M40, and M160 models.

M7i

The M7i router is Juniper Networks most compact routing platform.The M7i is ideal as an IP/MPLS provider edge router in small POPs or as an enterprise routing solution for Internet gateway or branch aggregation.It supports either 2 fixed Fast Ethernet ports, 2 fixed Gigabit Ethernet ports, or 1 fixed Gigabit Ethernet port via a Fixed Interface Card (FIC), as well as supporting 4 ejector-enabled PICs. The M7i router supports interface speeds of up to OC-12c/STM-4 and Gigabit Ethernet.

M10i

The M10i router is the Juniper Networks's most compact and cost-effective fully redundant M Series edge router.The M10i supports 8 ejector-enabled PICs via 2 built-in Flexible PIC concentrators, and interface speeds up to OC-12/STM-4 and Gigabit Ethernet.

M120

The M120 delivers support for 128 Gigabit Ethernet subscriber ports, with 10 Gigabit Ethernet or OC 192 uplink capabilities.It is capable of supporting MPLS services at Layers 2 and 3, including Layer 3 VPNs, the M120 is designed to deliver superior redundancy and facilitate the transport of legacy Frame Relay and ATM traffic over high-bandwidth Ethernet links.

M320

The M320 is a high performance, 10 Gbit/s-capable, distributed architecture edge router. It offers up to 16 OC-192c/STM-64 PICs per chassis (32 per rack) or up to 64 OC-48c/STM-16 ports per chassis (128 per rack), with up to 320 Gbit/s throughput.It also supports provider edge services in 10-gigabit POPs with the ability to support up to 32 type 1 and type 2 PICs and up to 16 type-3 PICs for 10 Gbit/s uplinks.PICs are compatible with M40e, M120, T320, and T640.

Comparison

Platform	M7i	M10i	M40e	M120	M320
Aggregate Half-Duplex Throughput	10 Gbit/s	16 Gbit/s	51.2 Gbit/s	120 Gbit/s	320 Gbit/s
FPC Slots	1 built-in	2 built-in	8 FPC slots	4 FPC slots	8 FPC slots
Full Duplex Throughput per Slot	4 Gbit/s additional 1 Gbit/s for FIC	4 Gbit/s	3.2 Gbit/s	10 Gbit/s	20 Gbit/s
PICs per Chassis	4 plus 2 additional fixed FE, or 1 fixed GE ports	8	32	16	32
Chassis per Rack	24	9	2	4	2
Redundancy	No	Yes	Yes	Yes	Yes

The Juniper M Series products are widely used in the large networks around the world.

Features

Features and services supported in M Series routers include advanced IP/MPLS edge routing services, a broad array of VPNs, network-based security, real-time voice and video, bandwidth on demand, rich multicast of premium content, IPv6 services, granular accounting etc. These IP/MPLS M Series Multiservice Edge Routing platforms are deployed at the edge of provider networks, in small and medium cores, and in peering, route reflector and data-center applications.

A single M Series Multiservice Edge Routing platform can provide a single point of edge aggregation for thousands of customers over any access type — including ATM, Frame Relay, Ethernet and TDM and at any speed from DS0 up to OC-192/STM-64 and 10 Gigabit Ethernet.

It also supports Layer 2 virtual circuits, Layer 2 VPNs, Layer 2.5 Interworking VPNs, Layer 3 2547 VPNs, VPLS, IPSec, GRE, IP over IP and other tunneling mechanisms.

It supports multiple levels of granular Quality of Service per port, per logical circuit (DLCI, VC/VP, VLAN), and per channel (to DS0) for traffic prioritization. These comprehensive QoS functions include classification, rate limiting, shaping, weighted round-robin scheduling, strict priority queuing, weighted random early detection, random early detection and packet marking. For network convergence applications, Layer 2 CoS can be mapped to Layer 3 CoS on a per DLCI, per VP/VC, or per-VLAN basis.

It also supports highly scalable J-Protect filtering capabilities, unicast reverse path forwarding and high-performance rate limiting for industry-leading DOS attack protection. The J-Protect security capabilities of the M Series platforms can be further enhanced with the Adaptive Services PIC, hardware that accelerates additional network-based security services such as high-speed NAT, stateful firewall with attack detection, DPI/IDP capabilities and J-Flow accounting. The M Series routing platforms have fulfilled the criteria for ICSA Labs Corporate Firewall Certification Version 4.0. ICSA Labs, an independent division of TruSecure Corporation, tests and certifies over 90 percent of security technology products in the world.

Juniper T-Series

Juniper T-Series

Date invented	1998
Manufacturer	Juniper Networks
Type	Network Router
Processor	Internet Processor

Juniper T-Series is a series of core routers designed and manufactured by Juniper Networks. The T-Series core router family comprises the T320, T640, T1600, TX Matrix, and TX Matrix Plus, designed for high-end and core networks with throughput from 320 Gbit/s to 25.6 Tbit/s with a maximum forwarding rate of 30.7 billion pps. The JCS1200, the industry's only independent control plane scaling system, brings virtualization to the core of the network. The T-Series, with the new TX Matrix Plus, provides transport scale up to 25 Tbit/s. The T-series routers run the JUNOS operating system.

Models and platforms

The Juniper T-series routers which consists of T320, T640, T1600, TX Matrix and TX Matrix Plus has thousands of units deployed by the major telecom and ISP networks around the world.

T320

The T320 has a total throughput of 320G bit/s (bits per second), compared with the bigger version T640's 640G bit/s. T320 Core Router is designed for use where rack space is at a premium and a wide range of interface speeds are needed. Each T320 router can support up to sixteen 10-Gbit/s ports (OC-192c/ STM-64 or 10-Gigabit Ethernet) while allowing lower speed connectivity down to channelized increments within the same chassis. Befitting its edge aggregation role, the T320 also can accommodate smaller interfaces. Those include ATM (Asynchronous Transfer Mode) and SONet (Synchronous Optical Network) interfaces at OC-3 (155M bit/s) and OC-12 (622M bit/s), as well as Gigabit Ethernet. For those connections, carriers can reuse interfaces from the M series and install them in the T series blades.

T640

The T640 supports up to 8 OC-768c/STM-256 ports, 32 10-Gbit/s ports (10-Gigabit Ethernet or OC-192/STM-64), 128 OC-48c/STM-16 ports, and an industry-leading 320 Gigabit Ethernet ports. It delivers up to 640 Gbit/s of capacity with the ability to forward up to 770 million packets per second (Mpps).

T1600

The T1600 delivers up to 1.6 Tbit/s of capacity (100 Gbit/s/slot) with the ability to forward up to 1.92 billion pps. The packet forwarding and switching complex of a T1600 supports 100 Gbit/s per slot. Current interface configurations include up to 16 OC-768c/STM-256 ports or 64 10-Gbit/s ports (10-Gigabit Ethernet or OC-192/STM-64).

TX Matrix Plus

Juniper's TX Matrix Plus is the central switching and routing element that can interconnect up to 16 T1600 chassis into a single routing entity with 128 slots and a sustainable throughput rate of up to 25 Tbit/s (30.7 billion pps). With TX Matrix Plus, operators can build systems containing up to 16 line card chassis for a total of up to 1024 10-Gigabit Ethernet ports or 256 40 Gbit/s ports. Using the virtualization capabilities of JCS1200, this available resource can be partitioned into aggregation or edge routing, or into the support of virtual service networks for advanced partitioned services such as video, mobile, and all corporate traffic.

JCS1200

The Juniper Networks JCS1200 Control System is the industry's first purpose-built, control plane scaling platform, providing high-power processing with a multi-CPU, multi-core server-class computing environment. With scalable memory and storage media, JCS1200 provides up to 12 routing engines in a compact one-quarter rack chassis.

Features

The T-series features include MPLS Differentiated Services (DiffServ-TE), point-to-multipoint label-switched paths, nonstop routing and in-service software upgrades (ISSUs), hierarchical MPLS, and service delivery coupling with the Juniper Networks JCS1200 and the Partner Solution Development Platform (PSDP).

Platform	T320	T640	T1600	TX Matrix with 4 x T640	TX Matrix Plus with 16 x T1600
Throughput	320 Gbit/s	640 Gbit/s	1.6 Tbit/s	2.5 Tbit/s	25.6 Tbit/s
Maximum Forwarding Rate	385 Mpps	770 Mpps	1.92 Billion pps	3 Billion pps	30.7 Billion pps
Rack Space	1/3 rack	1/2 rack	1/2 rack	3 racks	11 racks
10-Gigabit Ethernet Density	16	32	64	128	1024
Fully Redundant Hardware	Yes	Yes	Yes	Yes	Yes
Multichassis Capable	No	Yes	Yes	Yes	Yes

See also

- http://www.juniper.net/techpubs/hardware/t-series.html
- http://www.juniper.net/us/en/products-services/routing/t-tx-series/

Software router

Software router

Software router is a term denoting a computer or a PC designated to do the task of routing packets between networks. Because real hardware routers are costly (in most cases costlier than an average PC), this technique of modifying the PC and using it as a router is desired. The changes include but not limited to attaching two or more NICs network interface cards, to connect different networks,upgrading the current hardware such as installing additional memory modules etc.

See also

- Computer network
- Router
- List of router or firewall distributions

Juniper J-Series

Juniper J-Series

Manufacturer	Juniper Networks
Introduced	2004
Type	Network Router
Processor	General-purpose CPU

Juniper J-Series is a series of enterprise routers designed and manufactured by Juniper Networks. They are modular routers for enterprises running desktops, servers, VoIP, CRM / ERP / SCM applications. The J Series routers are typically deployed at remote offices or branch locations. These Services routers include the J2320 and J2350 for smaller offices, the J4350 for medium-size branches, and the J6350 for large branches or regional offices.

Platform development history

Juniper began working on J-Series in the middle of telecom downturn (2002), while looking for ways to extend its product portfolio. The main idea behind the new product line was to create the cost-optimized routing system that could utilize increasingly powerful general-purpose CPUs and operate under fully-fledged, multi-threaded OS. This was a major departure from "traditional" branch router design, which dictated the use of low-end RISC CPUs working under simplified operating system with marginal multitasking and memory protection capabilities. The first iteration of J-Series design was based on high-end Intel CPUs and featured Intel IXP-based interface cards running over PCI bus. Later models added PCI Express connectivity as well as specialized Cavium security processors. From the software perspective, J-series runs JUNOS with a real-time extensions for the forwarding plane function. This unique architecture allows J-series to avoid the "resource starvation" problem commonly seen on legacy software forwarding platforms.

Models and platforms

The J-series of routers includes the models such as J2320, J2350, J4350 and J6350. The initial models were J2300, J4300 and J6300 routers.

J2320

The J2320 routers are entry level service routers which gives up to 600 Mbit/s throughput performance, has four built-in Gigabit Ethernet ports.It has three PIM slots for additional LAN/WAN connectivity, Avaya VoIP Gateway, and WAN acceleration. They are used for one or two broadband, T1, or E1 interfaces with integrated services.

J2350

The J2350 router which has 4built-in Gigabit Ethernet ports , gives up to 700 Mbit/s performance.It gives five PIM slots. They are usually used for multiple broadband, T1, or E1 interfaces with multiple integrated services.

J4350

The J4350 enterprise router gives up to 1 Gbit/s in performance. They are usually used for DS3, E3, and Metro Ethernet interfaces with integrated services. It has six PIM slots. Two of these slots are enhanced-performance slots that provide additional performance to multiple Gigabit Ethernet configurations.

J6350

The J6350 gives up to 2 Gbit/s in performance. It has six PIM slots for additional LAN/WAN connectivity, Avaya VoIP Gateway, and WAN acceleration. These routers have optional redundant power supplies for high system availability.

Features

The J-series routers run on Juniper's network operating system, JUNOS. These routers have 4 on-board GigE ports and expandable WAN and LAN interfaces via pluggable modules. They have a wide range of interfaces supporting Serial, T1/E1, FE, DS3/E3, ISDN, ADSL2/2+, G.SHDSL and Gigabit Ethernet and a wide array of Layer 2 access protocols including Frame Relay, Ethernet and Point-to-Point Protocol (PPP)/HDLC. Other features includes Network Address Translation (NAT), and J-Flow accounting and advanced services such as IPv6, MPLS, Stateful firewall, Quality of Service, multicast, VPN, security services and IPSec. Juniper partnered with Avaya to deliver packet voice functionality.

J-Series routers directly benefit from modular and fault-protected software design of the JUNOS operating system. Unlike traditional enterprise routers, each software module in the JUNOS operating system runs independently and therefore cannot impact other other processes. The unique, generalized

JUNOS architecture provides complete separation of the routing and packet forwarding engines in platforms with both hardware and software forwarding planes. Even under DDoS attack, J-Series routers retain complete control over system operation, allowing console-connected operator to add new filters and policies in order to mitigate the threat. Parts of J-series technology were later reused in SRX series products.

See also

- http://www.juniper.net/us/en/products-services/routing/j-series/

Juniper E-Series

Juniper E-Series

Manufacturer	Juniper Networks
Type	Network Router
Processor	Internet Processor

Juniper E-Series is a series of Broadband Services routers or edge routers manufactured by Juniper Networks. The E series was originally developed by Unisphere Networks, which Juniper acquired in 2002. These routers provide multiple services including broadband remote access server, broadband video services, dedicated access, 802.11 wireless subscriber management, VOIP, internet access, security services, network address translation (NAT) etc on a single platform.The carrier-class architecture of E-series routers allows to combine Broadband Remote Access Server (B-RAS) and dedicated access capabilities (T1/E1 and above) on a single and integrated platform. The E-series routes runs on JUNOSe software compared to other series of routers of Juniper which runs on JUNOS.

Models and Platforms

The Juniper E-series includes six different models that are designed to address the variety of Service Provider requirements. The specific models include the high-capacity E320 BSR and ERX-1440 platforms, the mid-range ERX-1410 platform, compact ERX-710 and ERX-705 platforms, and the highly compact ERX-310. All E-series platforms use a single version of the JUNOSe operating system, and support a full suite of Internet routing protocols, including BGP-4, IS-IS, OSPF, and RIP.

E120

The Juniper E120 router is a high-performance router used primarily for small to medium-sized points of presence (PoPs) and central offices. The E120 has a 120 Gbit/s switch fabric and hosts up to six line modules that support OC3/STM1 through OC48c/STM16 and 10 Gigabit Ethernet rates.

E320

The Juniper E320 router is a high-performance router used primarily for large points of presence (PoPs). The The box supports a 100 Gbit/s or a 320 Gbit/s switch fabric and hosts up to 12 line modules that support OC3/STM1 through OC48c/STM16 and 10 Gigabit Ethernet interfaces with the ability to support 96,000 subscribers. The E320 was designed with video in mind, adding the quality of service (QOS) and high availability that carriers want for IPTV, as well as a huge increase in density. Cisco Systems has two boxes selling into this space: the 10000 series, considered Cisco's primary B-RAS entry, and the 7600 line of edge routers (of which the 7613 is the largest), which include some B-RAS capabilities. The B-RAS Backplane Switching Capacities of E320 supports up to 320 Gbit/s compared to 256 Gbit/s of Cisco 7613.

ERX310

The Juniper ERX310 is a compact but high-performance router that has a 10 Gbit/s switch fabric, two slots dedicated to line modules, and supports up to OC12c/STM4 and Gigabit Ethernet interfaces. The 3-slot router contains a 10 Gbit/s switch fabric /route processor (SRP) and the rest of the two slots dedicated to line modules.

ERX705

The Juniper ERX705 is a compact router that is used for small and medium-sized circuit aggregation applications. They can be configured with a 5 Gbit/s or 10 Gbit/s switch fabric (optional switch fabric redundancy), has five slots for line modules, and supports up to OC12c/STM4 and Gigabit Ethernet interfaces. These 7-slot router contains either a 5 Gbit/s or 10 Gbit/s switch fabric / route processor (SRP) with optional SRP redundancy for high availability and 5 slots dedicated to line modules.

ERX710

The Juniper ERX710 is mainly used for medium-sized and large circuit aggregation applications. They have a 5 Gbit/s switch fabric with optional redundancy, five slots for line modules, and supports up to OC12c/STM4 and Gigabit Ethernet interfaces. The ERX-705 and ERX-710 routers utilize the same line modules and I/Os used across the entire E-series product line.

ERX1410

The Juniper ERX1410 is an edge router that is used for large circuit aggregation applications. They have a 10 Gbit/s switch fabric with optional redundancy, 12 line module slots, and supports up to OC12c/STM4 and Gigabit Ethernet interfaces.

ERX1440

The Juniper ERX1440 is a high-performance router is used for small to medium-sized points of presence (PoPs). The ERX1440 has a 40 Gbit/s switch fabric with optional redundancy, 12 line module slots, and supports up to OC48c/STM16 and Gigabit Ethernet interfaces.

Features

The ERX system uses a modular, carrier-class design with a passive midplane, active front-insert line modules, and high-reliability, rearinsert input/output (I/O) modules. All chassis types use the same line modules and I/O modules. The 7-slot and 14-slot systems support full redundancy and line module hot-swapping to optimize network uptime.

The E-series JUNOSe system software and applications supports stateful Switch Route Processor switchover capabilities. The high availability for subscriber management applications, including all Point-to-Point Protocol and Dynamic Host Configuration Protocol access options, means that all subscriber sessions and services remain active during failure.

These routers maintain an entire routing table per port, which removes the route processor from the forwarding path and provides wire speed performance IP traffic streams, a process aided by Juniper developed ASIC technology.

The E-series supports subscriber management features in order to effectively aggregate traffic from access multiplexers, terminate Point-to-Point Protocol (PPP) sessions, and enforce QoS policies on a per flow and per subscriber basis. Features includes support for DHCP, PPPoE, PPPoA, PAP, and CHAP, domain parsing based on destination domain, IP address pooling, L2TP, LAC, LNS, RADIUS-initiated disconnect, RADIUS server support, auto-detection, Zero-Touch configuration, and TACACS+ etc.

The E-Series Modules supported are Channelized T3, Channelized OC3/STM-1 and OC12/STM-4 LM, Fast Ethernet/Gigabit Ethernet Line Modules, OC-3/STM-1 and OC-12/STM-4 ATM Line Modules, OC3/STM-1, OC12/STM-4 and OC48/STM-16 Packet over SONET Line Modules, Service Modules and IPSec Service Module etc.

See also

- http://www.juniper.net/us/en/products-services/routing/e-series/

Juniper MX-Series

Juniper MX-Series

Manufacturer	Juniper Networks
Type	Network Router
Processor	Internet Processor

Juniper MX-Series is a series of Ethernet Services routers designed and manufactured by Juniper Networks. These are a line of Ethernet-optimized multilayer packet processing devices designed for aggregation at the service-provider edge. These routers run on Juniper's network operating system, JUNOS. The MX960 platform is the industry's largest-capacity Carrier Ethernet platform, with up to 2.6 Terabits per second (Tbps) of switching and routing capacity. . In October 2009, MX-series was updated with new fabric and 120Gbps/slot linecards based on "Trio" chipset. Second-generation MX series routers are known as MX 3D [1]

Models and Platforms

MX 80 3D

The MX80 3D Ethernet Services router is the smallest member of MX family, featuring small form factor and one Modular Port Concentrator (MPC) with 80 Gbit/s capacity

MX240, MX240 3D

The Juniper MX240 Ethernet Services Router has a performance of 200+ Gbps throughput, scalability, and reliability in a space-efficient package.

MX480, MX 480 3D

The MX480 Ethernet Services Router is mainly used for dense dedicated access aggregation and provider edge services in medium-size and large Points of Presence (POPs).

MX960, MX960 3D

The Juniper MX960 Router is a high-density Layer 2 and Layer 3 Ethernet platform for several service provider Ethernet edge scenarios. The MX960 provides a range of Ethernet services, including VPLS services for multi-point connectivity. The MX960 is 14-slot router with 480 Gbit/s throughput in performance. A 40-port Gigabit Ethernet "dense port card" (DPC) and a four-port 10G Ethernet DPC were the initial line card modules, with Trio-based 16x10GE linecards reaching the full-duplex 120 Gbps [2] capacity.

Features

The MX Series is a family of high-performance Ethernet Services Routers with powerful switching features and are designed for high-performance service providers and enterprises. The MX Series has advanced MPLS, Multicast, Quality of Service, low latency and security capabilities. It provides flexibility and reliability to support advanced applications and services, including high-speed transport and VPN services, next-generation broadband multiplay services and high-volume Internet data center internetworking.

MX960 router include a switch control board (SCB), a routing engine and a Flexible physical interface card (PIC) Concentrator (MX-FPC). The SCB provides the switch fabric and control board functions, and acts as a carrier for the routing engine. The routing engine is similar to the routing engine for Juniper's T-series and M-Series routers. The DPC is a single-wide interface card that supports a maximum of four 10 Gbit/s packet forwarding engines. The Dense Port Concentrators (DPCs) provide multiple physical interfaces and Packet Forwarding Engines (PFE) on a single board that installs in a slot in the MX Series routers.

The 14 open slots on the MX960 router holds 12 line cards and two SCBs in a non-redundant configuration while it holds three SCBs and 11 line cards in a redundant configuration. Two routing engines with a 1.3 GHz/1,331MB version and a 2 GHz/2,048MB options are available.

The MX960 supports up to 16,000 VLANs per packet-forwarding engine. On a per-box basis, the MX960 supports 16,000 MPLS Label Switched Path head-ends, one million IPv4 and IPv6 routing-information base entries, one million IPv4 and IPv6 forwarding-information base entries; 25,000 Virtual Private LAN Services (VPLS) labels; 500 Open Shortest Path First (OSPF) sessions, 500 Intermediate-System-to-Intermediate-System (IS-IS) adjacencies, and 100 Label Distribution Protocol (LDP) sessions and 4,000 Border Gateway Protocol sessions.

Juniper Networks and Nokia Siemens Networks have joined in an agreement to offer their carrier customers an end-to end Carrier Ethernet solution with the solution that includes Juniper's MX-series Ethernet Services Router, NSN's A-series Carrier Ethernet Switch and the ASPEN "single click" network management system.

See also

- http://www.juniper.net/us/en/products-services/routing/mx-series/

HERMES-A/MINOTAUR

HERMES-A/MINOTAUR

HERMES-A/MINOTAUR is an Internet-to-Orbit gateway (I2O) which is a device capable of routing information between information processing systems in earth orbit and information processing systems (like computers) connected to the public planetary network (internet) via radio waves or even laser signals. It became online since June 6 2009, and was presented in the UN-OOSA Symposium of Small Satellites for Sustainable Development in Graz, Austria on September 8, 2009. It was built and operated by the Ecuadorian Civilian Space Agency on Ecuadorian territory, has a reported reception range of 22.000 km centered around the coordinates Lat: 2° 09' 28" S Long: 79° 53' 08" W

OSI model compliance

HERMES has no Terminal Node Controller (TNC), its main job is to convert protocols from one network in the ground (internet) to another network or device in orbit by routing and translating the radio or laser waves to a protocol that can be understand for user-end TNCs, it also has full remote ground station operation capabilities, but in modes like Delta, no control interface is needed. HERMES will serve transport, session and presentation layers, application layer will remain on the user side.

Operation

The HERMES-A/MINOTAUR gateway can operate in 4 modes, digital and analogical:

- MODE A (Alpha): Reception of data from orbit and relay trough Internet
- MODE B (Beta) : Uplink/downlink full duplex connection between computers on the Internet and orbiting spacecrafts
- MODE C (Gamma): Half duplex voice conversation between any computer on the Internet and manned spacecrafts
- MODE D (Delta): Automated APT/HRPT signal relay from weather satellites to any computer on the Internet

The MINOTAUR antenna array is the primary sensor, it is a 36 feet tall dual polarity, variable frequency resonator operating from 1.2 Mhz to 2.4 Ghz, is reported to have a 130dB gain, while the GORGON-B is the secondary array operating in VHF narrow band.

The MINOTAUR array has 2 ip cameras, one on-board and one outside, pointing to the array at http://minotaur.exa.ec/

Use

On February 5, 2010 the near miss between an Iridium 33 debris and the pico satellite Swisscube made evident the need of this kind of devices when the HERMES-A/MINOTAUR gateway was used by the Ecuadorian Air Force and the EPFL team controlling Swisscube to track the satellite signal over the internet in real time to monitor if the collision was to happen, due the coordinates of the would-be collision point was under HERMES-A range of operation.

A novel use of this device is the A SATELLITE IN CLASSROOM program which makes use of the Delta operation mode for giving access to meteorological satellites to elementary schools via internet so students can work the satellite images in real time.

ZTE ZXR10-Series

ZTE ZXR10-Series

Date invented	2001
Manufacturer	ZTE
Type	Network Router
Processor	Internet Processor

ZTE ZXR10 series is a series of Network Routers designed and manufactured by ZTE. The ZXR10 Series router family comprises the T8000, M6000, T1200, and T600.

As one of the world-leading data communications device provider, ZTE always considers data communications product as one of its strategic products. In 2000, ZTE took the responsibility to undertake National 863-300 core router research, and it successfully made the first high-end router with self owned property in China, which for the first time breaks through the monopolization of import high-end router. Focusing on the latest technology and market demands, ZTE based upon its powerful R&D strength and rich experiences in network operation introduces full series of ZXR10 routers and BRAS products. So far, all these products have been extensively used on worldwide market.

Core Router

T8000

ZXR10 T8000 is the typical Cluster Core Router, with the largest switching capacity in the world. T8000 cluster will support high-speed network access to more than 1 million users simultaneously. ISPs should benefit from less expensive, higher-capacity broadband Internet infrastructure.

M6000

ZXR10 M6000 is the first "Reconfigurable" router in the industry introduced by ZTE. By realizing reconfigurable service, hardware and software, it is the optimal device for IP/MPLS network, which completely satisfies the increasing network development and service diversification.

Broadband Multi-service Router

T1200&T600

ZXR10 T1200/T600, two models of reconfigurable carrier-class BMSG product made by ZTE, provide both SR and BRAS services on the same hardware platform. Featuring sound reconfigurable services, ZXR10 T1200/T600 are able to meet user's different requirements in different network construction stages.

See also

- http://wwwen.zte.com.cn/en/products/wirelines/bearer_network/

CE router

CE router

Customer Edge router (**CE router**) is a router located on the customer premises that provides an Ethernet interface between the customer's LAN and the provider's core network. CE routers, P (provider) routers and PE (provider edge) routers are components in an MPLS (multiprotocol label switching) architecture. Provider routers are located in the core of the provider or carrier's network. Provider edge routers sit at the edge of the network. CE routers connect to PE routers and PE routers connect to other PE routers over P routers.

See also

- PE router

ASR9000

ASR9000

The **ASR9000** is a router built by Cisco Systems, and is intended for Service Provider market.

The major characteristics are:

- From the ground up designed for Metro Ethernet networks
- Designed for Video and other High Bandwidth applications
- Supports a variety of interface types, those commonly used by Service Providers
- Uses IOS-XR, a full-featured OS

History

In the past, networking equipment was categorized as either a Switch or a Router, where a switch bridged L2/Ethernet traffic, and a router forwarded L3/IP traffic. As products became more sophisticated, the distinction between a switch and a router became blurred, as high-end switches were being designed to, in addition to bridging, to route traffic as well, and likewise routers were being designed to do L2 switching also. At the same time, it was becoming clear that the needs for the Enterprise market were diverging from those of the Service Provider market. Though still maintaining the terms Switch and Routers in their product names, Cisco divided their high-end networking products into those aimed for the Enterprise market and those aimed for the Service Provider market. In reality, many Enterprise customers use equipment Cisco categorizes under the banner of Service Provider, and vice-versa.

Prior to the introduction of the ASR9k, Cisco's high-end SP product portfolio consisted of the CRS-1, the GSR, and the 7600 (and the 6500). The ASR9k fits well within this product portfolio; it is the logical successor to the GSR. When the CRS-1 is deployed in a large network at the core, the ASR9k complements it on the edge; both run IOS-XR.

IOS-XR Release Support

Date	Release	Details
2008	3.7.2	Initial release of ASR9k
2009	3.7.3	
2009	3.9.0	
2010	3.9.1	
2010	4.0	

Article Sources and Contributors

Router *Source*: http://en.wikipedia.org/?oldid=390667075 *Contributors*: Jasonfward

Cisco IOS *Source*: http://en.wikipedia.org/?oldid=389190149 *Contributors*: Liberty Miller

PE router *Source*: http://en.wikipedia.org/?oldid=364452358 *Contributors*: Xeysx

Netgear *Source*: http://en.wikipedia.org/?oldid=389103370 *Contributors*: DRS1973

Gateway (telecommunications) *Source*: http://en.wikipedia.org/?oldid=383800020 *Contributors*: Helmoony

Wireless Router Application Platform *Source*: http://en.wikipedia.org/?oldid=389502259 *Contributors*:

Cellular router *Source*: http://en.wikipedia.org/?oldid=389719542 *Contributors*: 1 anonymous edits

Vyatta *Source*: http://en.wikipedia.org/?oldid=390594292 *Contributors*: 1 anonymous edits

Router clustering *Source*: http://en.wikipedia.org/?oldid=337263468 *Contributors*: 1 anonymous edits

Passport Carrier Release *Source*: http://en.wikipedia.org/?oldid=378753227 *Contributors*: Xeno

Core router *Source*: http://en.wikipedia.org/?oldid=369937032 *Contributors*: 1 anonymous edits

WAAV, Inc. *Source*: http://en.wikipedia.org/?oldid=374332287 *Contributors*: Chris the speller

Routing control plane *Source*: http://en.wikipedia.org/?oldid=356915654 *Contributors*:

Forwarding plane *Source*: http://en.wikipedia.org/?oldid=380511406 *Contributors*: Keithathaide

Turing switch *Source*: http://en.wikipedia.org/?oldid=357765887 *Contributors*: 1 anonymous edits

Nexus Hawk *Source*: http://en.wikipedia.org/?oldid=381504212 *Contributors*: DennisIsMe

Gaming router *Source*: http://en.wikipedia.org/?oldid=278780594 *Contributors*:

Untangle *Source*: http://en.wikipedia.org/?oldid=389754728 *Contributors*: 1 anonymous edits

Timos *Source*: http://en.wikipedia.org/?oldid=373774323 *Contributors*: Woohookitty

Netgear FVS336G *Source*: http://en.wikipedia.org/?oldid=355438067 *Contributors*:

Junxion *Source*: http://en.wikipedia.org/?oldid=383614770 *Contributors*:

NetHope NetReliefKit *Source*: http://en.wikipedia.org/?oldid=382513011 *Contributors*:

Juniper M Series *Source*: http://en.wikipedia.org/?oldid=390675052 *Contributors*:

Juniper T-Series *Source*: http://en.wikipedia.org/?oldid=370208500 *Contributors*: Μάριος Ζηντίλης

Software router *Source*: http://en.wikipedia.org/?oldid=383262179 *Contributors*: 1 anonymous edits

Juniper J-Series *Source*: http://en.wikipedia.org/?oldid=384864672 *Contributors*: Lightmouse

Juniper E-Series *Source*: http://en.wikipedia.org/?oldid=384868765 *Contributors*: Lightmouse

Juniper MX-Series *Source*: http://en.wikipedia.org/?oldid=387426896 *Contributors*:

HERMES-A/MINOTAUR *Source*: http://en.wikipedia.org/?oldid=359418020 *Contributors*: Twilsonb

ZTE ZXR10-Series *Source*: http://en.wikipedia.org/?oldid=357772036 *Contributors*: Last Emperor

CE router *Source*: http://en.wikipedia.org/?oldid=369991032 *Contributors*: Malcolmxl5

ASR9000 *Source*: http://en.wikipedia.org/?oldid=387610318 *Contributors*: WereSpielChequers

Image Sources, Licenses and Contributors

File:Ciscosystemsrouteratcern.jpg *Source*: http://en.wikipedia.org/w/index.php?title=File:Ciscosystemsrouteratcern.jpg *License*: GNU Free Documentation License *Contributors*: Coolcaesar

File:Juniper srx210 front view.jpg *Source*: http://en.wikipedia.org/w/index.php?title=File:Juniper_srx210_front_view.jpg *License*: Creative Commons Attribution-Sharealike 3.0 *Contributors*: User:MarcPG

File:Leonard-Kleinrock-and-IMP1.png *Source*: http://en.wikipedia.org/w/index.php?title=File:Leonard-Kleinrock-and-IMP1.png *License*: Public Domain *Contributors*: Leonard Kleinrock

File:Linksys WRT54GL.jpg *Source*: http://en.wikipedia.org/w/index.php?title=File:Linksys_WRT54GL.jpg *License*: Public Domain *Contributors*: User:J4ckzor

File:OpenWRT 8.09.1 LuCI screenshot.png *Source*: http://en.wikipedia.org/w/index.php?title=File:OpenWRT_8.09.1_LuCI_screenshot.png *License*: GNU General Public License *Contributors*: User:Moxfyre

Image:Netgearlogo.svg *Source*: http://en.wikipedia.org/w/index.php?title=File:Netgearlogo.svg *License*: unknown *Contributors*: transfered from

Image:Green Arrow Up.svg *Source*: http://en.wikipedia.org/w/index.php?title=File:Green_Arrow_Up.svg *License*: Public Domain *Contributors*: AutisticPsycho2, Dbenbenn, Juiced lemon, Korg, Multichill, Pagrashtak, Redrose64, Trisreed, ZeroOne, 17 anonymous edits

Image:Netgear router1.jpg *Source*: http://en.wikipedia.org/w/index.php?title=File:Netgear_router1.jpg *License*: Creative Commons Attribution-Sharealike 2.5 *Contributors*: Caroline Ford

Image:Netgear ProSafe 8 Port Gigabit Switch GS108 front.jpeg *Source*: http://en.wikipedia.org/w/index.php?title=File:Netgear_ProSafe_8_Port_Gigabit_Switch_GS108_front.jpeg *License*: Creative Commons Attribution-Sharealike 3.0 *Contributors*: User:Zuzu

Image:Netgear ProSafe Dual WAN VPN Gigabit Firewall FVS336G front.jpeg *Source*: http://en.wikipedia.org/w/index.php?title=File:Netgear_ProSafe_Dual_WAN_VPN_Gigabit_Firewall_FVS336G_front.jpeg *License*: Creative Commons Attribution-Sharealike 3.0 *Contributors*: User:Zuzu

Image:Cisco-rs1.jpg *Source*: http://en.wikipedia.org/w/index.php?title=File:Cisco-rs1.jpg *License*: GNU Free Documentation License *Contributors*: GreyCat, Josette, Siebrand

Image:Cisco-VIP-2-40-hdr-0a.jpg *Source*: http://en.wikipedia.org/w/index.php?title=File:Cisco-VIP-2-40-hdr-0a.jpg *License*: Creative Commons Attribution-Sharealike 3.0 *Contributors*: User:Adamantios

File:Cisco-Gigabit-Switch-Router-Performance-Route-Processor-0a.jpg *Source*: http://en.wikipedia.org/w/index.php?title=File:Cisco-Gigabit-Switch-Router-Performance-Route-Processor-0a.jpg *License*: Creative Commons Attribution-Sharealike 3.0 *Contributors*: User:Adamantios

Image:Turingswitch.png *Source*: http://en.wikipedia.org/w/index.php?title=File:Turingswitch.png *License*: Creative Commons Attribution 3.0 *Contributors*: User:Telecomtom

Image:Netgear ProSafe Dual WAN VPN Gigabit Firewall FVS336G opening.jpeg *Source*: http://en.wikipedia.org/w/index.php?title=File:Netgear_ProSafe_Dual_WAN_VPN_Gigabit_Firewall_FVS336G_opening.jpeg *License*: Creative Commons Attribution-Sharealike 3.0 *Contributors*: User:Zuzu

Image:Minotauro-laser.jpg *Source*: http://en.wikipedia.org/w/index.php?title=File:Minotauro-laser.jpg *License*: Attribution *Contributors*: Ecuadorian space agency

CPSIA information can be obtained at www.ICGtesting.com
Printed in the USA
LVOW051554300412

279727LV00005B/90/P

9 781242 981944